CACTUS
IN THE
WILDERNESS

Don't Waste Your Life Feeling Unloved

SHARON R. LEIPPI

CACTUS
IN THE
WILDERNESS

Don't Waste Your Life Feeling Unloved

Balboa Press books may be ordered through booksellers or by contacting:

Balboa Press
A Division of Hay House
1663 Liberty Drive
Bloomington, IN 47403
www.balboapress.com
1 (877) 407-4847

Because of the dynamic nature of the Internet, any web addresses or links contained in this book may have changed since publication and may no longer be valid. The views expressed in this work are solely those of the author and do not necessarily reflect the views of the publisher, and the publisher hereby disclaims any responsibility for them.

ISBN: 978-1-9822-0493-8 (sc)
ISBN: 978-1-9822-0492-1 (e)

Library of Congress Control Number: 2018906240

Print information available on the last page.

Balboa Press rev. date: 05/17/2019

BALBOA
PRESS
A DIVISION OF HAY HOUSE

CONTENTS

Introduction

Notes

INTRODUCTION

Are you feeling lonely and discouraged ?

Like a prickly cactus, in the wilderness ?

Don't waste your life feeling unloved.

Yours should be a life of happiness and joy. Jesus died on the cross – in your place – to present you blameless.

You are blessed !

You are loved !

1. The Wilderness

Jesus was in the wilderness for forty days (Mark 1:13) NIV.

2. Jesus is Always With You

Jesus will be with you in the wilderness. Jesus is omnipresent and can be in many places at the same time. You won't be alone.

God is with you in your wilderness. Psalm 23:4 (NIV)

3. Connected to the Church

Being part of a community of faith and worship has been such a positive experience.

So many life groups to join and so many people to meet !

The mid-week study was enjoyable, and I especially liked the church's hiking life group.

I feel loved when I'm at church.

4. Renounce Your Lack of Forgiveness

Forgiveness is necessary.

This has been a challenging one for me. Forgiving is easier if you can look at the situation with humor. Just discussing forgiveness makes it easier.

"For if you forgive others their transgressions, your heavenly father will also forgive you. But if you do not forgive others, neither will your Father forgive your transgressions."

Matthew 6:14-15 (TLV)

5. Stay Focused

Keep your mind on Christ.

When driving, I always have my radio tuned to the local Christian radio station. Throughout the day, the positive and encouraging tunes replay in memory.

"I've worked up such a hunger and thirst for God, traveling across dry and weary deserts."

Psalm 63:1 (MSG)

"I bless you every time I take a breath."

Psalm 63:4 (MSG)

6. Choose Christ Now

Make a choice.

Get off the fence.

Choose Christ, who loves you !

Give your life to Jesus Christ – He is the Messiah.

"He is the way and the truth and the life."

John 14:6 (NIV)

"Those who did not have their name written in the book of the living were thrown into the lake of fire."

Revelation 20:15 (GNT)

7. God Loves You

YHWH loves us all so much that he sent his son, Jesus, who came down to Earth, born in Bethlehem.

Jesus is real ! Jesus is the savior. Yahusha HaMashiach became the lamb, taking our sin, shedding His blood and dying on the cross, in our place, so that we might have life everlasting.

"Anyone who believes in the Son has eternal life. Anyone who does not believe in the Son will not have life."

John 3:36 (NIRV)

"But unless you repent you will all likewise perish.

Luke 13:3 (RSV)

"If you declare with your mouth, 'Jesus is Lord,' and believe in your heart that God raised him from the dead, you will be saved."

Romans 10:9 (NIV)

NOTES

Intro & front cover: young saguaro cactus growing out of the rock (Sweetwater Preserve in the Foothills of the Tucson Mountains)

Introduction: cardinal (Catalina State Park, Arizona)

Chapter 1: saguaro cactus (Catalina State Park);
saguaro cactus & mesquite tree with mistletoe

Chapter 2: prickly pear cactus & wildflowers;
Christmas cholla cactus & chain cholla cactus

Chapter 3: wildflowers in Catalina State Park;
barrel cactus (Big Wash Trail) & hiking life group from Resurrection Lutheran Church, 11575 N. First Ave., Oro Valley, Arizona 85737

Chapter 4: pincushion cactus (Catalina State Park);
snow-covered Yucca cactus (Feb. 22, 2019, Tucson); prickly pear in background

Chapter 5: Catalina State Park

Chapter 6: Tucson, Arizona

Chapter 7: ocotillo cactus & prickly pear cactus (Tucson, Arizona)

Notes: saguaro cactus

Books: Catalina State Park

Back cover: saguaro cactus (Catalina State Park)

Books by Sharon R. Leippi:

Fire & Ice: ALASKA – Baked, Blended, & Sautéed
A gluten-free, dairy-free cookbook, also corn-free, with Alaskan
photography from over thirty photographers.
(Frosty Books – 2012 – hard cover)

Think Hope Live: Embracing Life – Defeating Suicide
The focus is on suicide alertness, and suicide prevention.
Part of the book is for the down-and-out, and *Think Hope Live*
will hopefully give hope to the reader to keep on living.
(Balboa Press – 2017 – soft & hard cover and e-book)

*Road Tripping from Alaska to New York City: Journaling the
Journey and Taking Pix Along the Way*
Traveling on the road with a pet, including photography and some history.
(Balboa Press – 2018 – soft cover and e-book)

Ubiquitous: Apple Juice, Lemon Juice, Olive Oil
A worldwide natural remedy of apple juice, lemon juice, and olive oil.
(Balboa Press – 2018 – soft cover and e-book)

Big, Bad Poetry: Biggest and Baddest in the West
Humorous poetry.
(Balboa Press – 2019 – soft cover and e-book)

About the Author

The author and her cat, Chopper, live at Regina, Saskatchewan in Canada, where Sharon enjoys growing vegetables, berries, and flowers in her one-third acre garden at Davin, on the family farm that dates back to 1899.

Printed in the United States
By Bookmasters